"Mike Jurkovic is either the William Carlos Williams, Allan Ginsberg, or Charles Bukowski of the Hudson Valley. Reflecting their influences, his work is drawn from his unique blueprint, the poems built of his singularly barbed brick and mortar. Grounded in reality, *AmericanMental* spews beauty, humor, and rage at the sublimely monotonous. One envisions the poet spent, under a Bodhi tree with a tall drink - a blue Buddha shaking his head in disbelief, as *all the psychosis slides east on Thursdays* watching *us thicken with laughing eyes.*" Read this "*cry from the fist*, throw back your head and shout!"

-Janet Hamill's, *A Map of the Heavens: Selected Poems 1975-2007,* was recently published by Spyuten Duyvil

"*AmericanMental* gives us a poet at the top of his game. Iconoclastic impulse wrestles progressive idealism in the town of shit-lorn. Here we confront pettiness, inequality & desperation as felt by many who've had the misfortune of believing in that American Dream: success for all & everyone, only to find it doesn't exist. That's not to say life is perfect elsewhere. No. These poems challenge hypocrisy & injustice wherever found. Crack the cover – a rousing ride awaits!"

-Roger Aplon, Editor/Publisher Waymark - *Voices of the Valley*; author *Barcelona Diary, It's Only TV*, and, from Unsolicited Press: *Mustering What's Left - Selected & New Poems 1976 - 2017*

"He's the mad house jester whose jabs jolt and sting. As one of his poems puts it, *gravity gets us all,* which is as serious as it gets. Enjoy this work, it is original and a pleasure to read."

-Guy Reed, poet, *The Effort to Hold Light, Second Innocence*

AmericanMental

Poems by Mike Jurkovic

Luchador Press
Big Tuna, TX

Copyright ©Mike Jurkovic, 2020
First Edition 1 3 5 7 9 10 8 6 4 2
ISBN: 978-1-952411-15-1
LCCN: 2020937820

Front cover art: Greg Correll
Author photo: Mom
Back cover art: Mike Jurkovic
Back cover photo: Tim Tomlinson
All rights reserved. No part of this publication may be reproduced or transmitted in any form or by any means, electronic or mechanical, including photocopying, recording or by info retrieval system, without prior written permission from the author.

Acknowledgments:

Buzzed - *Waymark* #12, 2019
Cameras rolling. Ratings high. - *Waymark*, #10, 2018
device – *Slipstream* #37, 2017
East 138 - *The Baltimore Review*, Spring 2005,
It Was a Nice Day – *Penny Ante Feud* #10, 2012,
    Petrichor Review 2013
Marty's 81 - *Chronogram*, May 2019
Nephrite Jade – *Such An Ugly Time, Rats Ass Review*, 2017,
    11/9 Fall of American Democracy Anthology, 2017
oblong thing - *Packingtown Review*, 2020, *Conclave*, 2020
Pale Diaspora – *The South Carolina Review*, 2006
Passing Shower – *Work Zone*. 2012, *Passager*, 2012
Ping Pong – *Reflecting Pool: Poets & The Creative Process*
    (Cod Hill Press, 2018)
Scholars hence - *Panolopyzine* 2018
small time stuff - *Chronogram*, September 2019
still life w/mandolin – *Platform Review*, Spring 2017
the haloes in her glasses – *Waymark, Voices of the Valley*, #6
the irreversible future - *Panolopyzine* #12, May 2019
the night unfolds (Remy and Nina) - *ponder review* #1 V.2 2018
topeka – *Home Planet News* #5 2018, *Long Island Quarterly*, 2018
Turn The Blue Corner - *Calling All Poets* 2020 Anthology
    (CAPS Press, 2019)
We Spend Much of Our Lives in the Way – *Main Street Rag*, 2016
Like Light, Bright Hill Press 25th Anniversary Anthology, 2018

TABLE OF CONTENTS

Sudden stop. / 1

Marty's 81 / 3

Turn the Blue Corner / 5

we all leave who we were and become who were are / 6

We Spend Most of Our Lives in the Way / 7

rude impact / 8

Cameras rolling. Ratings high / 9

topeka / 11

the manic gulls of Liverpool / 12

Folk Singer / 13

the night unfolds (Remy & Nina) / 14

Albert's Riddle / 16

Cloudland / 17

the gold engraved / 18

Can Man / 21

Scholars hence / 22

small time stuff / 23

syringe drop / 24

bragging rights / 25

Nephrite Jade / 26

East 138 / 28

the haloes in her glasses / 30

Clearing House / 32

Pale Diaspora / 33

device / 34

It Was a Nice Day / 36

Still life w/mandolin / 37

Passing Shower / 39

Buzzed / 41

She controls the Ambien / 43

Two Wives Ago / 45

Two Doors Down / 46

if the world finds us here / 47

Candy Machine (for eric) / 48

oblong thing / 50

Ping Pong / 51

the irreversible future / 52

Wonderland Parade / 54

because maybe / 55

Preacher Roe Confesses / 57

Chasing Hammers / 58

Tell Them, My Love / 59

Three Stools Down by the Ladies Room / 60

Brake light out / 61

Forward by George Wallace

In the first two lines of AmericanMental, PJ Pratz finds himself *in shit-lorn without a friend in the world and the towns folk know it.*

It's a town of paranoia, poverty, isolation, empty religion and futility; a grim place, laced with drugs, alcohol, Lotto. Lurking behind the scenes of the town's business-as-usual veneer and vapid flag-waving is a wasteland of dead end romances, tacky retailing and lucrative illegal trade. A town at the cruel nexus of a number of problematic cultural forces that warp 21st century America. A town where the American small-town dream has died and there was no post-mortem. A menacing place where *the cops know your whereabouts and the mayor has your wallet.*

Sound a bit stark or confrontational? Perhaps. But it shouldn't come as a shock. American literature has long had a love-hate relationship with small town culture ever since rising from our agrarian origins to become the world dominant, industrial giant. Ever since we stopped thinking we could go over the river and through the woods to get to grandma's house.

In the poetry of Edgar Lee Masters *Spoon River Anthology* we find ripped aside the mask of propriety in central Illinois, exposing small town pettiness, dereliction, dreams deferred and empty facades. In Sinclair Lewis' *Main Street* we are introduced to Gopher Prairie, an ignorant town of physical ugliness and smug conservatism. Sherwood Anderson's hapless citizens of Winesburg, Ohio try and fail to locate meaning, personal connection and love amid the town's elm-shaded streets.

Shirley Jackson provides the ultimate dystopian satire in *The Lottery,* portraying a small town that carries on an unexplained ritual blood-sacrifice every spring. William Inge's *Picnic, Come Back Little Sheba* and *Splendor in the Grass,* offer the unrelenting and painfully limited horizons of small town life. More recent authors from Don DeLillo to Steven King, and moviemakers from Larry McMurtry *(Last Picture Show)* to Martin McDonagh *(Three Billboards)* to the Coen Brothers *(Fargo)* have brought often lurid tales of small town life into the current dialogue.

It's a horror story, basically.

Where are the gods whispering in the corn and the wind? Where is the two fisted yeoman with his cap in hand and his generous head of hair waving back to heaven and the endlessly reverential sky, one with the valleys and prairies and plains of a free and brave continent?

Anyone who longs for the voice of rustling leaves in these works is more likely to encounter the rusted out cars and rumble of highway traffic leaving town in the long autumn of America's slow decline. And anyone who has actually dug his or herself a hole and become buried alive among the living dead of a small American town knows instinctively what Mike Jurkovic's on about.

It's not exactly a country for whole men.

And yet one senses that for all the vitriol, things are not so simple as they seem. That in fact, despite the harsh criticism being doled out in *AmericanMental,* there is for the discerning reader a testament to be made out of it… in the form of the life of a man who hates his whereabouts yet sticks around to tell the tale. Remains there to be its material and forensic witness of a pervasive and perilous socio-political kleptocracy that materially stiffens the necks of its debased residents.

Why would something like that even happen?

Chalk it up to our continued love affair – despite all the evidence – with the American dream. The small town American experience, which once upon a time served as womb and engine to rugged and loving agrarian families, to independent, upright citizens, to wholesome supportive communities.

We've been taught to believe and to honor that dream. So when it comes up short, neither Whitmananian or Bunyanesque, but a wreck of itself, yielding stunted offspring and thwarted hopes, then what? When we discover that its citizens are caught in a prosaic dead-end waltz, that the business of America is DOA, what? That the writers trapped in the middle of it remain neither despairing nor completely alienated, but casting about with a cold inquisitive hard eye at what might have been and never was, lives lived as useless as a broke hammer?

It is a cause for hope. Despite the many critical novels, movies, music, poems and plays. Despite harsh first-hand accounts of the disappointments which is America 2020. Despite the relentless probity in *AmericanMental*, we retain in our hearts the great notion of what American small town might yet be. But not where *good guys don't get far" "a quiet town, sunny and white, where Kalashnikovs make wealth/and Lotto governs the poor.* In the big equation, it doesn't measure up to our expectations, but there is solace in bearing witness to its shortfalls. And by virtue of that, a reminder of the palpable resilience of the American dream.

The fact is, if you scratch the surface of a critic you find a romantic with redemption in his heart and quite possibly the romantic in yourself emerges. *AmericanMental* reminds us of our belief there may yet be something wonderful to redeem beneath all that rust and decay. The parade runs past/the halfway house and food pantry/

Where the soup is thin
Til the meds kick in
Then everyone swings
In the holiday mood.

That's why we need to read these poems today.

George Wallace *is Writer in Residence at the Walt Whitman Birthplace, first poet laureate of Suffolk County, LI NY and author of 36 books and chapbooks of poetry, published in the US, UK, Italy, Macedonia and India. A prominent figure on the NYC poetry performance scene, travels internationally to perform and teach. Editor of Poetrybay.com, co-editor of Great Weather for Media, and editor of Long Island Quarterly and Walt's Corner, a weekly poetry column in The Long Islander, a community newspaper founded by Walt Whitman in 1838.*

to Emily, and all those working to restore

the work of revolution is in all our hands
-mj

Sudden stop.

PJ Pratz found himself
in shit-lorn w/o a friend in the world
and the townsfolk knew it.
They'd eaten his baleful kind before.

Now hold on. I'm not trying to color
the good people of shit-lorn
as zombies. We have TV for that
and our own aspirations. Our own silent prayers
in good times and bad.

The fine folk of shit-lorn
have just been hoodwinked y'see
by a life w/few known headstones
heralding greatness. Grey carved letters
abrading away.

Why do you think that is?
How have we failed
or have we? When you think about
All the times
We quote the Bible
and our founding fathers
You'd think we'd be
a perfect nation

But no. We fall in line
like father knows best. Gilligans
in fifty year mud singing songs. Singing songs
when people are dying all around us.
The water, the air, the food we congest.
A pratfall. A plunge into meekness
not long forgotten. If history remains,
after we go.

Marty's 81

Marty's 81, has a parched, post-pneumonia cough
and the shits from diverticulitis. A blood clot in his leg
he can't afford the apixaban for
cos you can't survive on a pension and social security.
Lives w/his daughter in a shit-lorn town in the Hudson Valley
that everyone struggles to avoid lest you're
driving through in a funeral procession
because his third wife *Peg, a beautiful girl, a very smart girl,*
took to the booze n the old farm house they'd rehabbed
somewhere in shit-lorn, Pennsylvania.
28 years. He counts. 28 years.
Played Carnegie Hall as a child
and sang *doo-wop w/the mafia boys*
back in Bensonhurst. Bought his first Vette in '59.
A turquoise baby that stole your breath
while Sal The Snake stole your wallet.
Shows me pictures on his cell phone.
His whole life in his hands. In the hands of strangers.
The old stone house he restored w/Joan, his second wife
who *had five kids and took on my three.*
Plays piano for Saint Margaret's
down the road in shit-lorn at the intersection where
the light don't work. The '62 Corvette. The '65.
People were worth something then he rasps,
cold phlegm seizing his pipes.
Shows me his cousin Maury's place up in Saratoga.
Raises horses and runs a marina on Manhasset Bay.

Maury's the smart one he swears scraping his lungs.
More pictures of grandkids and horses, cars and pianos.
His fix-it shop in shit-lorn where
he still fixes vintage stereo equipment.
I take in a piece here a piece there he says for pocket money.
I tell him about my McIntosh w/the fried left channel.
Here's my email, send me some pictures maybe I can help ya
he says. Served in the service *but that don't mean shit.*
His son's got his hunter green '74 Vette until he can get
a place of his own. Pictures of his daughter's daughter
who just turned four. *Gonna start her on scales
when the cough's all gone. Any day now,* he says.

Turn the Blue Corner

Caught in the rhythm
of the Great American Thimblerig
I find myself shuffling shells
for the tourists from Wisconsin
Who missed their bus
and now they're here. On Avenue C,
Where all the psychosis
slides east on Thursdays
Asking themselves
or someone else
or someone
just as fucked
If the two drink minimum
applies to them.

Everything pertains in New York
I say. So throw some hot sauce
on that plain cheese pizza
and watch carefully.
The night remains sleepless
and it makes no difference
What language the ole lady yells
when she wanted
Ranch, you asshole! Not hot sauce!

we all leave who we were and become who we are

we all leave who we were and become who we are
with the noose not far behind. nipping at our heels.
we all leave who we were and become who we are
behind mountains, like love always does.
we all leave who we were and become who we are
escaping down streets where the fate of fever and skin
tingles in the rain. our sixth sense seeking tequila.
we all leave who we were and become who we are
and threaten revolution. then watch from the sidelines
as the oil men fight back

w/Raphael Kosek & Will Nixon

We Spend Most of Our Lives in the Way

We spend most of our lives departing.
Disrupting the whole human flow.
Stuck in our tracks, our whereabouts,
our lovers, our lies.

We spend most of our lives in the way
and our lack of clairvoyance defines us.

We spend most of our lives walking idly.
Waiting for a wise man or a pretty girl
to sweep us away. Out of the line
of fire. Away from traffic. Away from
the broken politics cluttering the hall.

rude impact

you fall from the bardo into this
shakedown. this realm of fraud and
spite. where the North looks South
w/brown skins picking the white skin's salad.
you fall from the bardo into this
un-mannered situation. this crude hive
of monsters on the morning commute.
you fall from the bardo hoping to
retain or relearn some form of grace and
charity. but it's futile. all you can hope for
is immunity. then feign ignorance
like all the rest.
you fall from the bardo
back into this.
good luck.

Cameras rolling. Ratings high

Two doors down
from the revolution
I'm licking war wounds
w/a vodka sting,
When the general
w/her reality show
puts me on the kill list.

Feeding the banking clan
from the hireling's platter,
she lays waste my periphery.
Wants something from me
I just don't have. Truth. Gospel.
An inkling. Some belief that somehow
we'll get past this dreamless time.
This querulous point of cruel debate.

Like a drone adorned in a negligee
who can't dance Tchaikovsky
so cranks up the Stones,
Insists her boss needs to know.
But I ain't tellin'
no matter how many
digits I lose.

*This ugly crusade's
gone on too long*
she swears, bearing down on me
w/a cleaver. Cameras rolling.
Ratings high.

topeka

I never did get back to Topeka.
What was the point? There were pipe bombs
in every direction. Just like here.
Up n down. Forward, back.
Horizon to horizon. Moon to moon
n Grandma's down eight fingers n falling
into her chili n chips as Pop Pop swears at Quick Draw
and little Lena gets off the bus n walks into
the dim lit, dimwit, gimlet, gin house that
only the brave defy. Which is why I'm here.
Hiding behind happy hour. My religion lost
and my faith failing fast. Each dark minute
hauling itself forward. Towards the water.
Towards the morsel. Towards the dead legends
I call my own and number myself
among. We jump off in droves.
The chasm yawning. The darkness rushing by.
Just grow soldiers they say,
reminding me a lot of what I heard
back in Topeka. Where prairie winds
blow rust and water mains burst
just like that. Just like everywhere else
neglected by its people. Dismissed as a political problem
when, in fact, it's a culture. A question of folklore
and the lack thereof. No present. No past.
No holds barred when it comes to demise
and the dollars it makes. Squalor. Contempt.
A breed I've indebted myself to. A ruined lineage.
Just like Topeka.

The manic gulls of Liverpool

The manic gulls of Liverpool
implore their team to triumph.
Alert the cops to wrong side parking
Tweet, twonk, doo dee doo.
Carry the news. The hymns of St. Luke's.
Herald the garbage men.
Welcome, wheel, and bid adieu.
Drown out the reconstruction.
Proclaim the reconstruction.
Laugh like children. Cry from the fist.
Sing choir. Go solo. Echo the homeless.
Live in the limelight. Dive bomb nuns.
Steal your lunch. Punch your budgie.
Browbeat pigeons and small dogs.
Mimic our rudeness. Our crude dialect.
Joke of extinction. Watch us thicken
w/laughing eyes.

Folk Singer

After 40 on the day shift
60 pounds and Type A
Everyone's a folk singer
in shit-lorn. Am Dflat E

To the fitful despair of friends and exes,
They've returned to their guitars and tambourines
w/a vengeance. Gflat Cflat D
Chord slash C7
The lights go up. First set finished.
Two doubles down, diminished.
The untethered roam
to the new salon
Everyone's hoping to play
cos they stream you live
Bflat Bflat G   A A Am

B9 A D. B9 A.D.
Clap. Clap. Clap.
Next on the list
Gm.

the night unfolds *(Remy & Nina)*

the night unfolds
like Simone rising
from Sartre's lap
And we're left alone
watching, from our hovel
east of theirs. It was so rare to see
them cohabiting intimate corners
like this: He holding her book,
she holding his.
We giggled at their dalliance,
their feral talks along Montparnasse
and dark carafes of wine.
Reviewing detours, before and after
and how the crossroad crisis
costs us all in the end: The girl, the train.
the day. The ellipsis and apothecary.
The moment and its time.
Fascists rally. Soldiers invade.
Havoc ensnares. Innocents die.
Did you hear that? Innocents die.
Even those on the periphery
doing radio for the Vichy
or arguing symmetrically
for the gulag and free will.
We overheard them over
our macarons and sauvignon.

For a day in Paris
is always
a day in Paris
it just depends what side you're on
and how history's cold deceits
blow far beyond the Seine.

Albert's Riddle

The world is a curious madhouse - Einstein

The world's a fuckin' nuthouse, man!
Don't bullshit me. Every motherfucker thinkin'
he's the king of the hill
and do you know the firearms
needed to defend that? The powder, rocket,
and anelace? The IED and Judas Cradle.

Couldn't you say something more heartening
like *That's why they put erasers on pencils* *
or *The meaning of life is to go back asleep
and hope tomorrow is a better day*
like ol' Charlie Brown, that bald little lotus,
worries each worrisome day.

Seriously dude,
give it some thought.
Even Plato practiced dying.
So why this innocuous axiom
from a brain so cock-sure as to ask
who has the fish?

Who has the fish?
Didn't you ever
drop a line in a creek
and watch the day go by?

*Bob Murphy, beloved NY Mets radio/TV announcer (1924-2004)

Cloudland

I came upon a man
bruising himself w/stones.
The orange king decrees it!
he cries. The gravel cutting
his skin. His blood pooling
at the base of the foot of a wall.
*It's meant to keep us in
not them out!* I told him or
tried to tell him
above his chanting. But his children
soon joined in. Then his church and
union hall.

As the king's men stake their claim
we assemble at potters' field
in colorful rags, but
an army sharing selfies
soon defeats itself.

I've tried real hard
to keep politics
out of this but I can't.
We either advance each day
or we don't 'n some
will fall 'n some will turn
'n some will make the mountain top.

the gold engraved

If you awoke
fragile today
steer clear.
I'm standing
on the dry line
gathering steam
And may say things
I don't mean
or purport
to have
written.

Hitch my hide
to the pity parade
and parrot
its opiate
shuffle.
Barely disguise
my disgust
for the words
you choose
to screed
your codex.

Your rabid
holy verse.
Your clown's
redress
And how
it persuades
the querulous few
to shoot me
on sight.
Your sucker
theorems

Historical
record.
Your family
portrait
beside FDR,
his cousin,
And the black guy
you've fingered
to demean
and deplore.

You piece
of shit.
You
rat's ass.

You
hellbent
blind soldier
At war
against
science.

At war
Against
ourselves
In which
no house
stands.
Not even
the gold
engraved ones.
Not even
the gold
engraved.

Can Man

Bent by the weight of deposit,
Can Man pushes through shit-lorn
w/a beard like the guys in ZZ Top.
And I know by the way he sets his aim
he knows napalm and Hodgkins.
He knows the crying of '68
When it all went to shit just days after
Maggie said yes and Jimi broke his brain.

That damn guitar! That damn guitar!
That's all I heard. He said low w/a machete scrape.
Tacking forward for a beer can, he straightens slowly
like a Mekong morning. *I didn't get Hendrix, I admit*
Not until after he died and the blood pooled everywhere.
Especially at home where it didn't sink into the addled soil
but left footprints on broken, Bronx pavement.

Too late he says *to fret*
But you're not absolved.
We gave them our shit w/o consequence
And that's the fuckin' truth
no matter how history calls it.
That's the fuckin' truth and the terms
of our surrender.

Scholars hence

It's an apocalyptic feel,
isn't it? As we carry our shit
like it makes any difference
in the rockets' red glare.
Conventional. Thermal. Celluar.
Take your pick. Place your bets.
Either way we fall. Leaving it to
the scholars hence
to examine our umbrage.
Our shit. Our shit. It's always
our shit left behind no matter how vengeful
the flood. How concussive our personal weaponry.
Our shit
and the
sermons.
Our shit
and the channels
devoted to it.
Our shit
and the lack
thereof.

small time stuff

Shit always falls they say
so pardon my umbrella. It's my only strategy
at the moment 'cos

I'm feeling tapped out. Like the words are hard to say
and my command of them fades like
mists ascending Mohonk.

Poof. All gone.
Only the language of failed obligations
in my mouth, my

gluttonous mouth of happenstance and krill.
Small verbs sculpted by fate
into

smaller stuff. A tarnished fringe.
The sin being sadness
and how we atone.

syringe drop

The new initiative for downtown shit-lorn
is to install syringe drops in every public restroom.
Keeps the litter off the streets the mayor magistrates
and you find yourself thinking that
Maybe hell is the day after
you snap awake back in the box
you chose to lie in. The door's locked.
The mud hardened. A small elm has taken root.
A parking lot is planned. A trombone from the nursing home plays
One of your old favorite songs from way back when
and you find yourself thinking

bragging rights

I got the infant caskets for a steal
at the auction at McNulty's,
The funeral parlor I grew up next to
in shit-lorn. Where dreams tank
and basement made buzz bombs
go off by the hour leaving six dead
plus nine from yesterday's shooting.
And even though business is good,
the old man had to sell it for a kidney
'cos good guys don't get far
in shit-lorn. They don't even get bragging rights.
'Cos when so much goes untended
in a land of surveillance
The smallest mercies
go unserved.

Nephrite Jade

I may not be the brightest bulb
but I know it's a shell game
which, by high definition, is a con we should
all be used to and on the orange alert for
given the nature of politics. Given our propensity
for swindle. Our eagerness to take
each other to the cleaners and turn
the same trick over n over
in the name of democracy. Freedom,
The intentional perversity of truth.
The circumnavigation of fact, fiction,
and the pursuit of happiness.
I mean what's more sleight of hand than voting?
Like Ancient Greece. Like old New York.
Sharps play the urban decay. Stoke the diaspora.
Stalk the unwashed and un-imagined.
Voting. Fey! It's a gesture at most.
Nothing conclusive. A tally the big boys ignore
cos they know better or at least they say they do
and we believe. Bereft of higher ground,
they meet our standards. Exceed expectations.
Give birth to new devils. Say our voice matters
then punch mute.
What's it gonna take, huh? How much of how little
do you want them to divide? Despoil? Maraud and plunder?

There's gotta be a breaking point. Everyone has one and
thus too, each mob. Must we resign to camps and
shit in dark holes? Our children and elders
their soldiers and whores,
pushing their product down the old Silk Road.
Over the grand peaks we once called our own
until they blew them up for coal and passage.
And we marched in line. Our burden, their trade.

East 138

Through our debris
Our children walk
Barefoot in barrios
Burdened at birth,

Cry the cold china
Billboards in Harlem
East 138
I still call you home.

Turn back the promise
The premise, the menace
East 138
I still call you home.

Abandoned like babies
Burnt and begotten
Over a river of peril
Standing alone,

At the crossroads, a beggar
Of jade and Jehovah
Hustlin' for handouts
From shadows long stilled,

Spit out the devil
The demon, the donor,
The monster, the baby
The shrill of the dead,

Run the cold plasma
Over hordes of the faithful
East 138
I still call you home.

the haloes in her glasses

Trish McGyver
had a sinister tic.
A lithium logic
that begged dedication.
Her mercy flew in fragments
and she made a darker jazz
w/a set degree of fixture
and no sliding scale,
that dates back to sixth grade
when I stole my first kiss.

The sun was bright that day.
The air unseasonably clean.
The Christmas lights haloed
in her glasses. I couldn't resist.
I took her right there. Mouth to mouth.
Miss Norton flustered. We were two of a kind.
Desire an un-tempered skill.

Prone to the mad calls of profit
our hearts locked perfectly. And all through college
we plotted our motive. Sold pot to raise funds.
Took our first shipment of Armalite Colts
and a box of Berettas. Then we read,
in the Armed Tribune, about a new arms maker:
Glock. It was '63: The Beatles on the BBC.
I saw here standing there w/haloes in her glasses
and proposed.

We invested heavy. Under the table.
Across the boards. Across the Da Krong River
w/freedom in the hull. Then she miscarried
and we took a break. Sailed Greece. Made connections.
Made some calls and flew to Taiwan. Nairobi.
We never talked of kids again.

We went low profile in the eighties
but it didn't last long. We were one of a kind
so we went to Nicaragua. Detroit. Camdem. Newburgh.
Selling cheap and plentiful to both sides. Cops. Robbers.
Makes no diff. Everyone's gearing up for survival.

War unabated. Abroad. At home. To avoid bloodshed
we vacationed on private islands. Even after retiring,
we got involved deep w/the Middle East. Fattening kings,
killing their house. That income set us up to this,
our friends and family all in one room,
bearing flowers to her grave.

Clearing House

I never could find a good use
for acoustic shadows so I'm
putting it right here next
to northing west. After twelve years of transfer
from notebook to napkin to notebook
a comic dance of retrofit has found its charnel ground.

Vague pronouncements is another orphan
successfully placed and please
Welcome to the page the noir flicker
where my head used to be.

Have you heard the one about
the clock doctor who stops me in the street
thirty-eight years to the day of his first house call,
To tell me how he cured the chimes in my father's
grandfather clock by removing my porn
from the pendulum's arc?

No, probably not because I just made it up. I do that
from time to time with wild corpuscle abandon.
Because having been such previously
my personality shards are all smoothed over.
No edge. No glare. No backstage help
through the bankrupt sprawl where a capsized blonde
places her bets in the dead, dry dust of Juarez.

Pale Diaspora

I'm sorry I mistook the Mercedes Benz logo for a peace sign
But I haven't been myself of late.

Now I'm not writing this to make excuses for myself
Or leave the door open to any greater anti-testimony
from a senate of my peers but please welcome
the Lethargic Anarchists, who by their very nature
are the bulk of my acquaintances.
The password to their hearts is the title of their memoirs,
written each day, in a fine debtor's hand.
Not disenfranchised, but accomplices — silent and stealthy
Alert, on a moment's notice, to avoid complex intimacy
when a simple yes will do.

They bear me no ill but concede me my illness.
They hope for repair yet carry no tools.
 We share a common trial: Making strange heroes
 who leave post-its as referrals to our character;
 a smattering of truth that does not adhere.

device

It's been a while and my heart
and the vodka know it. How many times
you said no here. Goodbye here.
I hear the trains.
Their riders expecting normal
but not tonight. Tonight I have other plans
and they include immolation. Time dying.
Breath. Pulse. This rabid drill.

An eight ball thunders down my veins.
I've come back to redistribute the mayhem
and hand in my notice. Alerting you all
to my exhaustion. My firewall kilned by distress,
distrust, and detox. I'm off everything now and
feeling better than ever. Free to object
and make my argument louder than
your curbside chatter.

Device here. Device there.
One by the tracks n
one by the bridge n
one by the ER.
Some of us will make it
and some of us won't. But isn't that
the running joke behind
learning from the past?

We know there's a growing army like me
out there: Skirting the shadows.
Afraid of the day. And still we get on those trains
thinking we'll get home.

It Was a Nice Day

You never walk shit-lorn
the same way twice
and that's a great relief
for this clan of criminal lovers
whose teeth don't match.
Whose peevish complaints
annoy me.
Leave me
unattended.

I only blew up the building
because I could. It was a nice day.

I only blew up the building
because my back was up
against the wall
and I needed recreation.
Because I wanted to,
I had to. Because the line
between gang
and government
is gone

Still life w/mandolin

In this city
of tall women
intent on
getting somewhere
the bedlam is
built in.
The chaos concurrent
w/everyday life.

A-swirl in clouds
of estrogen,
I pilot my way
w/o getting hurt.
Murder and mayhem
engage my eye.
Salesgirls look at me
like I have six heads

which I do, by the way,
'cos I'm stoned 'n
trying to purchase
a book about flogging
w/credit long since
expired. And a smile discolored
from years of red wine.

A tall order
of diplomacy
is needed.
So I borrow fifty
from a chanteuse
who only knows
two songs 'n
sings them
over 'n over
Whenever
I'm trying
to read.

Passing Shower

I come from a long line of weathermen
who swore Noah's storm a passing shower.

As the last son before nine daughters,
all of whom shattered the glass ceiling
by founding girlweather.com,
I kept the website current.

Crazy weather was normal now
and getting worse. Mary swore
the extinction winter
was tomorrow.
Beth saw rain,
sad girl that she was.

Tina liked the lonely cool
of autumn. Molly, her twin,
loved upheaval. Kate married taut convolutions,
had four kids and didn't give a damn
how the wind blew.
Amber and Anita, the second twins,
loved the New York heat.
Salacious climes were Annie's bag,
I swear by sweat, she'd say.

Each one crazier
than a shit-house rat.
All except Mo',
who kept it real.
A-storm's a-comin
she'd fondly say.

Buzzed

In the universe next door to ours
I'm buzzed as fuck in a wormhole
chasing the North Pole's magnetic slide.
But it's picked up speed
so my compass can't be trusted.

In the universe next door to ours
old hippies don't get gout.
Eight million baristas and sommeliers
have better things to do
and better medical benefits. Confusion headaches
are a thing of the past.

In the universe next door to ours
Children float on gleaming tides.
War dead are not dishonored.
The last ship hasn't sailed
or suffers in dry dock.

In the universe next door to ours
the city isn't laced w/warheads.
Bomb trains don't rattle
the western shore.

In the universe next door to ours
I'm buzzed as fuck n free
of triggerfish and time stamp.
Everything fits! There's an Irish bar
on every corner
and I ain't comin' back.

She controls the Ambien

. . .and I'm okay w/that.
Someone's gotta. Be the
responsible party
I mean. I gave that up
sometime around '81
when Tampa Red expired
and Reagan won.
Walter Cronkite
said goodnight
and it's never been
the same really. Not for me
or anyone. That's why drugs
are so lucrative
over and under
the counter.

There are gunmen
and best picture. A recession
and daily drone strikes
in the Gulf.
A new computer and virus.
A cold war, a scandal, and
a test tube baby.
Icons die. Alone or usually
in sets of three. A neat little trio -
Hoagy, Marley, Pigmeat -
all gone to Heaven or wherever it is
artists go
when their labor's done.

And of course there's people
being born but, then, as now,
too many to service
or list here.
Unions strike. Hunger strikes.
More bullets.
Less food.

And like everything else
on this not new day
in a not new year
w/the roads torn up
and great cities torn down.
Earthquakes, drought and
baby killers. Mario and Israeli bombs.
Luke n Laura. Ali's last.
I could go on
but why?

Two Wives Ago

It's a beautiful thing. Stockpiled.
Vacuum sealed. Purchased a little each pay day
for the last fifteen years
and two wives ago. Neither could see
my reasoning so I gave up trying.
You can only save yourself in the end.
Everyone else drains your supplies.

Dated. Rotated. Each 50mm can
checked monthly for corrosion.
In this room mostly corn meal
and 50lb bags of sugar.
A tunnel to the highway
shelved floor to ceiling
w/corn and tuna.

In this room alone, my water.

Two Doors Down

There is no corner house
for your latest desire but there is
a cozy duplex, just off Main,
behind the shoe repair
and water department. Two doors down
there's a cute artisanal bakery
where cupcakes become dreams
and a toothless man rails for mince.

The Dutch Apple Chocolate
is sometimes dry. Other than that
it's a quiet town, sunny and white,
where Kalashnikovs make wealth
and Lotto governs the poor.
The ringleader lights his flaming hoops
as lost girls play hopscotch w/religion
in their earbuds.

The way is cleared for the prophet.
The riser erected. The carpet tacked down.
The faithful stampede. Bring their kids to the show.
Tomorrow could be the be all and end all
but it's still just a staircase, a footnote.
A cheap sleight of hand God sometimes uses
then overdubs strings. Then on Wednesday
the town board votes and on Thursday
another mass shooting.

- with Will Nixon

if the world finds us here

I suddenly understood her fear and
it was my fear too. fear the madness
will out. that night is not w/o end.
that this could be our last moment
if the world finds us here

Candy Machine *(for eric)*

They've come and gone
grown and died
These first children
of the last war. Their eyes bright
w/cinema dreams. Stopping, w/daddy's first nickel
for a packet of gum or
Walking right by to their seats
ignoring my mirrored veneer.
Never knowing I was
a direct descendant
to first century Egypt
And a mid-level guy named
Hero of Alexandria whose machine
swapped your bronze
for a spritz of water holy.

Now money in money out
may be the whole basis of our belief system,
But it wasn't mechanized
until London, 1883 when
Percival Everett, w/o direct lineage
to Hero the Gone but wise to the wants
of the people, pitched postcards and paper
for a Cartwheel Penny

But not me! Built to dispense
sweetness and salt
between cowboys and women in silk,
I became the place they all met,
giggled, gossiped and treated the girls
to chocolate almonds.

Sure some kicked me and shook me and cursed.
But over the years you let go and move on.
You have to. Or else the whole world becomes
a dark, dark place that even the magic screen
cannot illumine.

oblong thing

Twilight falls on Bygone Road
and the vague expected settles.
The vandals took everything
so Dylan was wrong.

Starburst arpeggios happen less
to children old enough to understand
That building is the labor of years.
Ruin, a thoughtless hour.

It was never my imagining
to leave you all the answers.
Bequeath you the rifles and prescriptions.
The shop-vac in the shed.

But entertaining angels
is an oblong thing. A fistful of chords
and unguarded splendor. Your first and last steps
stored in a cloud. In a cloud where Heaven
should be.

Ping Pong

I ping pong between machines
for what? To calibrate my steps
towards the dirt nap? To tend my cell,
my contusions? To email the news
of a fellow cognate's imminent promotion
from this warring plain?
Praying the bantam shifts
I've confessed
strike God's fancy
as alternate plans
to push the days forward,
not back because
falling from fucked
to fascism
wears you down.
Deletes your decorum.
Makes for uncivil discourse
and thus, this poem.

the irreversible future

We ooohed and ahhhed at the sixty-four World's Fair
and the droids that would take away our work and
give us more time w/the kids. More time to smoke. Read n watch.
Drink n fuck n fuck some more. Raw metallic arms did the work
of fifty men w/o unions and overtime. Hulking huge brains
sprayed pretty light and reasoned our equations.

The atom had no blowback. The Wonderful World of Chemistry
was just one pill ahead. We marveled at modems and picture phones.
Big oil gave us dinosaurs. The Happy Plastic Family heartened us all.
Different trips. Same monkey. Disney ruled the air.
Weather stations under the Arctic ice
would correct the world's climate.

The cities of the future had no ghetto
(that we could see) They were less sad and frantic
than those to come.
No one homeless. No one alone.
Jet Packs - oooh. Space stations - ahhh.
Deserts were farms. Dark robots picked the fruit.

The Mick was there I saw him. Amid the supercars, The Kennedys
w/o Jack (for the darkness did just dawn) We ooohed and ahhhed
zipping on the monorail carrying
our radiated nickels and dimes.

Or were they pennies? I forgot the poor.

We explored the mysteries of a woman's mind.
Wisconsin cheese! 3D led to 4G. Five.
They say we don't need six.

We ooohed and ahhhed and became.

Wonderland Parade

Expect delays on Main Street this Saturday
as the Winter Wonderland parade
winds past the Dollar Store
and Dunkin' Donuts. The laundry mat
and vacant shoppes. Past the OTB and liquor store.
The pay day loans and Dell's Garage.
The diner's serving hot cocoa.
The library's closed
till further notice.
The war memorial's overgrown
but we're hoping for snow that day.
You don't want to miss
St. Gemma's Choir
outside the Quiet Meadow Nursing Hime.
Past the pregnancy center and Good Will.
Walmarts. Rite-Aid. Candy canes and Santa.
Bing's will be hosting holiday songs
w/well drinks 2 for 1, 1 through 4.
The parade runs past
the half-way house and food pantry,
where the soup is thin
till the meds kick in
then everyone's swings
in the holiday mood
to the Master's lawn
where the lights shine bright
and a big inflatable Kevin
waves at us all.

because maybe

Live long enough and the plot becomes apparent. This is the
 only way
it could turn out: The fire roasted eggplant flat bread is
 running late.
The edible hasn't kicked in in time for the movie.
The wine lacks a certain weight and the folks at the next table
are ready to strangle each other.

Live long enough and life costs you an axle. Love hits the wall
more often than not and the rubbernecking results in muscle
 sprain
and hyphenated discs. The downward arc of history crashes on
 your lawn.
Corporate names become your own. Surly asides become
 convention.

Live long enough and people implore you to pray for them.
 Pray they be rid
their cancer and conceit. And you do because maybe they
 know something
you don't: That short of the nuclear option what else is there?
Strafe downtown? Torch town hall? Increase the valium and
 xanax?

Live long enough and the choice becomes abuse or entertainment.
Your dynamic points of interest dull. The sand becomes listless.
Tariff and sanction scintillate. You come to terms.

Live long enough and you tire of doing. This. That. Every little
   fuckin' thing.
But maybe that's how this shit-storm passes: In service to
   someone
in need. To someone mistaken as foreign. To someone you
   saw as stranger.
A careening penitent inclined to believe.

Preacher Roe Confesses

The queen of shit-lorn Day
looks at me like a lunch cart brimming
w/nachos, Busch Beer, and Chicklets.
Cuts my thumb then hers
swearing deference, roses and rescue.
Though our commerce and congress
a colorless thing, she still thinks me
the height of her memoir.

And maybe I am.
At least she looked up
from the binge back and text slope
And shared our regressions
over the best Chinese in shit-lorn.
While the fair rolled up and
Romans in the cheap seats
pelted me w/eggs

cos I know the cat's out of the bag
and breeding. They know I know
it's a fault line of fools
and the first tremors are apparent
in the Alpine glow of aftermath
Where the querulous games we pursue
have run their natural course.

Chasing Hammers

I'm chasing hammers
through a three-penny wind
Wondering what
they have on me? What somnambulate urge
have they deciphered? What call? What photo?
What misuse of time?

I despair of all this
but only of late.
What were once mere bouts of incubus
have amassed themselves
into a wrath of tinder.
Disrupt my walking hours
along a fault line of fools
seeking repose. Eclipsing the light
as matter of course. Scouring streets,
erasing my name.

Tell Them, My Love

If they ask, my dear
tell them I died behind the wheel
waiting for the light to turn,

Waiting for the ass ahead of me
to discover his left foot from his right.

Tell them, my love, I died simpering
while the road crew widened thoroughfares
smoothed the finish of my blackened heart.

Tell them, my love, should any be inclined to query
of my well-being, that I'm buried with the odometer,
the universal gear.

Tell them I withered in the heat.
The stewing froth of motion and mediocrity,
Prey to the rush and clatter,
the zooming zoom zoom of death.

Tell them, my love, I died in love.
With you, with them,
despite the miles between us

wishing I was home.

Three Stools Down by the Ladies Room

I found her in a bar
from fifty years ago
When we both shared this side
sharing beers.
Now the worn mahogany
split us as ghosts became
apparent: *You used to go w/what's her name
and I went w/that red headed guy.
Huey? Dewey? What was his name again?
Craig? Greg? Billy?* I threw out willy-nilly
Uncertain of my whereabouts
but damn sure I was being watched.
*Well anyway he gave you my Zeppelin ticket
so I punched you in the face. Over there,
three stools down by the ladies room
and what's her face came out and jumped on me
and the whole bar turned to watch.
Great times! Great times!* I assured her,
courting her need now that the ley lines
led back to here.

I got up as I had years before.
Her name was Wendy
was all I could say.

Brake light out

Sunrise comes to shit-lorn
and the sugar high passes.
The art house comes down
but the porn ghosts abide.
Humping. Pumping. Threesomes. Four.

Sunrise comes to shit-lorn
and nothing changes. Angry saints
bicker foul. Storm clouds hide
the horizon. Refuse. Rummage.
Sixteen rounds.

Sunrise comes to shit-lorn
and you can count the floss picks
on the street. The cops have your whereabouts
and the mayor's got your wallet.
Implode. Unplanned. Brake light out.

A 2016 Pushcart nominee, poetry and musical criticism have appeared in over 500 magazines and periodicals with little reportable income. Full length collections, *Blue Fan Whirring*, (Nirala Press, 2018); *smitten by harpies & shiny banjo catfish* (Lion Autumn Press, 2016) Chapbooks*: Eve's Venom* (Post Traumatic Press, 2014) *Purgatory Road* (Pudding House, 2010) Anthologies: *Reflecting Pool: Poets & the Creative Process* (Codhill Press, 2018); *Like Light: 25 Years of Poetry & Prose* (Bright Hill Press, 2018); *11/9 Fall of American Democracy* (Independent, 2017)); *Water Writes: A Hudson River Anthology,* and *Riverine: Anthology of Hudson Valley Writers* (Codhill Press, 2009, 2007) *Will Work For Peace* (Zeropanik, 1999). President, Calling All Poets, New Paltz, Beacon,, NY. Music features, interviews, and CD reviews appear in *All About Jazz, Van Wyck Gazette,* and *Maverick Chronicle*s 2018-present. Featured poet: London, San Francisco, NYC, Albany, Baltimore. Tuesday night host of Jazz Sanctuary, WOOC 105.3 FM, Troy, NY. Was a monthly contributor to *Elmore Magazine,* 2008-2016; *Folk and Acoustic Music Exchange,* 2003-2010; *Chronogram,* 2005-2007. His column, *The Rock n Roll Curmudgeon,* appeared in *Rhythm and News Magazine,* 1996-2003.

www.ingramcontent.com/pod-product-compliance
Lightning Source LLC
Chambersburg PA
CBHW030350100526
44592CB00010B/895